Sounding

Leah Ellen Marks
December 2, 1990 — December 7, 2007

Leah's sculpture, *Angel,* was to be a gift for her father.
Leah finished it a few days before the accident.
She never delivered it.

Photograph by Barry C. Altmark

Sounding

BY BARRY MARKS

Negative Capability PRESS

MOBILE, ALABAMA

Sounding

Copyright © 2012, Barry Marks

ISBN 978-0-94-254477-0
Library of Congress Control Number: 2012936882

Cover and Interior Design by Megan Cary
Edited by Patty Jameson

Angel, sculpture by Leah Marks; photo by Barry C. Altmark
Photo of Leah Marks courtesy of Barry Marks

Published by:
Negative Capability Press
62 Ridgelawn Drive East
Mobile, Alabama 36608

(251) 591-2922
negcap@negativecapabilitypress.org

www.negativecapabilitypress.org

This book is for and dedicated to those who are coping with the loss of a loved one—learning the difference between grief and mourning, struggling with the questions and unhappy with the answers, enduring the world and everyone in it who is not similarly suffering, and, perhaps against their will and preference, surviving.

It is for Lauren—the younger sister, doomed to forever be the other child, the bravest and strongest person of us all—who has managed against all odds to get up in the morning, brush her teeth, and go on with her life; and it is for Jennifer, half-sister/half-mother, who suffers silently and who goes on with a better life for her sister's sake. For you, there cannot be enough respect, compassion, or love.

Most of all, it is for Leah. Who deserved better. And it is, in sorrow, for the world that lost her, all that she was and all that she could have been.

TABLE of CONTENTS

GRAVITAS

I will get to the bottom of this.

What is most compelling
bends light,
bends time,
is so heavy within itself
it darkens a star

until no radiance,
no music,
no joy can escape.

How else to explain
these leaden hours
that echo your name,
the hollow weight
of your absence?

| I

What misery to be afraid of death.
     What wretchedness, to believe only in what can be proven.

— Mary Oliver, *I Looked Up*

LAY LAKE

How John and I are fishing,
despite everything.
Because of everything.

How you find bass
where the shore and the weeds
and a fallen log make structure.

How John has caught a bass
and I have not.

There is so much I would show you.

How the mist glides over Lay Lake
and two men,
the men who loved you,
the men who failed you,
sit in their little boat, one talking,
the other silent within himself.

How your name
is the only word I hear.

PHANTOM LIMB

You are not here
but I feel you.

That pretty much says it all.
Like hearing a cry
after the fall
and seeing only an empty place.

Like hearing after music
or seeing the sun
within one's eyes,
knowing beyond
the sense's lies
is knowing a lot
and knowing not.

I could say
        AND THEY LIVED HAPPILY
each reader would say
        EVER
            AFTER.

You, daughter,
are not here—
      you are   there
      where   ever
      there   is

not here, I know, but
where—
I do not know.

I do not know if
or how much
you hurt

just as I did not know
that you hurt so
many times.

I did not know;
how can any
father brother lover other
know how another
hurts?

Still, some phantom of pain insists:
She hurt
like you hurt
when you were hurt
like you were.

I felt so much for you
but I could not feel   for you,
to keep you

from having to feel the hurt
of a phantom father,
the horror in that last instant
when I cannot know what you felt
no matter how hard I try to punish myself;

and I want to die for you
as I want to die for you
but I cannot, I only feel for you

in the darkness that
will heal with time
but never grow back;
it is like I have lost
part of myself,

leaving only pain.

It is like that.

AND IT IS LIKE THIS
For Joe, Lee, and too many others

Grief has its own architecture,
sorrow its own physics,
the pain of loss, a set of principles
unlike any other.

It's as if there were a world
where magic is science and words
are the engine of chemistry:
this combination makes gold out of iron,
that one brings the rain and these words,
spoken in cadence, open doors

and the doors of grief line the halls
bisecting the brain.
Open one door and step into darkness
so heavy it swallows all light,
the next door sucks you in and down,
down until you bottom in a bottle or
between alien sheets:

Door of Fantasy.
Door of Memory.
Doors of Music, Disney, Favorite Foods—
            suspension of words that once
            made *Happy Birthday*
            what it was.
Door of Faith.

Listen. You will know you have free-fallen
into that other world when every loss,
however trivial, returns you to the great loss.
When you cannot remember
and cannot forget
the face,

when your dreams are release
and waking is torture.

Pilgrim, Novice, Apprentice to the Sorcerer of Sorrow,
as you are so was I,
as I am so shall you be.

Seek solace, answers, peace—
you will find only pain;
if you avoid
all doors,
you will live in a lightless hall of mirrors.

SHE

Who was smiling the last time I saw her.

Who leaned into me as we walked to the car
that used to be her mother's, the car
she loved and personalized with abuse.

Who was never without defenses but
loved me so unguardedly that day
it will carry me forever.

Who loved me that way because she knew
I needed it as much as she did.
Who was like that.

Who called six of her friends' parents
Mom or Dad
and made them feel she meant it,
because she did,
and whose friends,
maybe a dozen of them,
told me they were her best friend
and all were right.

Who bought her mother cigarettes,
enjoyed taking her sister to school,
and was equally proud that the one
knew she loved the work
and the other never would.

Whose cat came when she called.

Who was a con artist, a liar,
a storyteller, a thief of hearts
and a clown, all because
it gave people
what she needed them to have.

Who was self-taught and, at seven,
had a cheese omelet
waiting for me when I came home,
perfectly made
and ice cold.

Who could make a Who face,
talk like a cartoon,
do hinky-pinks for hours
and make her sister laugh
or cry with equal facility.

Who forgave me for thinking
she didn't care anymore
about getting candy from her dad
on Valentine's Day,
or at least tried to make him think so.

Whose first word was *Dadda*
and whose last words to me were *I love you*.

She said that the last time I saw her.
I did not know it would be the last time.

WHAT WAS LOST

At least the others can put up posters
on telephone poles if it is a dog,
or milk cartons and the Walmart board
if it is a child.

They can walk the neighborhood,
calling, empty leash in hand,
or go on local T.V. begging
for a miracle and later

for *closure*, as if that were a good thing.
At least for them there is more than
listening to sympathetic ramblings,
and collected idiocies of the kind:

> *You have another child, don't you?*
> *Be thankful for the time you had.*
> *God has a plan/needed an angel/loves you.*
> *My dog was like a child to me.*

and after a time, I suppose, the horror
turns to grief and guilt.
All things do, eventually.
Dust collects on the doll with blue eyes.
The dish outside the door fills with rain.

PERSISTANCE OF MEMORY

Like a swan, beautiful,
circling the placid mind's mirror surface.

Horrid voice,
violent temper
and furious workings beneath.

Like a swan.

Walk to it and fall through the glass.
Drown as she glides past.

What did you lose?
The infant, the child?
No, it was someone else
and someone that might have been.

Someone who could have
made your memories silent,
tamed them so that
they would not bite so hard.

SNOW DAY
1996

Leah and Lauren
build a house
out of cushions
from the love seat and sofa.

They bring treasures
to fill the rooms:

> *a Lambchop pillow*
> *a jewelry box*
> *dolls that have names*
> *and a few that do not.*

And still the snow falls,
now down, now side-ways,
enveloping the house, changing
the landscape, remaking the world.

We will cook soup today,
hearty with beef and cabbage
and crowd around the fireplace
instead of the T.V.

"This is my idea," Leah announces.
"Yes," answers Lauren, "it's my idea, too."

DIVORCE
2001

Now that you're old enough,
we can hurt you.

We confuse the issue of love
at the time you need to understand it most.

We say things like,

> "We still love each other,
> but we can't stand to be together."

> "Our forever is over but our love for you
> is unaffected."

> "People don't fall out of love—
> the magnet just turns around."

We look for you to act out.
(Boys, drugs, beer.)
All because you don't understand
that it is easier to sever than to retie
the Gordian Knot of marriage.

Now that you're old enough,
we ask you to understand these things
that we cannot fathom.

> *Children are like eggs*
> *and marriage like an onion.*

> *The one fragile,*
> *perfect,*
> *full of potential.*

The other peels away,
peels away
until nothing is left.
Except in our eyes.

It's unfair that I go on without you.
I will say I am sorry to you
for the rest of my life.

I UNDERSTAND

Leah, 2006

> *Moon has hidden her obsidian secret*
> *deep in the folds of Night.*
> *It glows darkly, calling to you.*

You yearn to fly,
floating effortlessly,
clothed only in night.

> *And you alone, Night's child,*
> *can release the secret, take it into yourself as*
> *Moon smiles, glows her approval.*

You yearn to burst from your flesh
and be more, to touch
every living thing with your mind.

> *Your parents are not flesh and blood,*
> *cannot be mere mortals. They are*
> *light and shadow, or perhaps*
> *hope and time.*

You are younger than the morning,
perfect as the dawn.
And utterly shocked
that the sun ever rises without you.

||

If, as I can't help suspecting, the dead also feel the pains
    of separation...then for both lovers...bereavement is a universal
        and integral part of our experience of love.

— C.S. Lewis, *A Grief Observed*

LIES

I should never have told her
that she didn't need to worry
if I should die before I wake.

I should not have said the puppy
was just sleeping by the side of the road
or that we gave away the hamster
or that I did not know
how her cat died in the fire—
I should have told her that its form
was outlined in soot by the side of her bed,
where he came to sleep with her each night.

They tell a father he has only one job
besides making money.
Don't drop the baby.
Fault, guilt, regret?
These are for mothers.

I rubbed her arm
and told her to go to sleep one last time.
I will never know if that
was the right thing to do.
If I cannot know that,
I will never know any truth again.

FATHER'S DAY

LITTLE TIME

1991, 2011

Little hands.
Eyes looking up from the blanket.
Midnight feedings with CNN.

Time stops.

Cruise missiles on Saddam.

My future,
your future.
All the time in the world.

Men don't have *Best Friends Forever.*
We don't buy matching bracelets.
We bond with other men over football
and with women over flesh.

The ways to our hearts
are through bellies or balls;
what is trapped there
rarely finds the way out.

But we will have time
for me to find
a way to know you.
Little hands. Little eyes.

Men, men, men.
Women, women, women.
I never saw myself in another's eyes
until I made yours.

I promised big things to those eyes,
better than I was promised:

Never to say to you,
"The hurt means it is getting better."
"You're old enough for your wants not to bother you."

Never to say,
"Not now,
I am too busy for you."

We had all the time in the world
to get to know each other, didn't we?
All the time to get it right.

I never told you, but I never had
a best friend.
I made one.
I will never have another.

Wait for me.
I promise I'll be there for you.
We will have
all the time
in the world.

ANGELS AND AIR

Bert is my best friend.
I hardly know him.
He cooks me chicken and dumplings.
He borrows my vodka.
I took him to my daughter's memorial—
he told me about his high school girlfriend.
She also died in a wreck.

Alex is my best friend.
We get loaded together and go to topless bars.
We watch football.

They live across the hall.
They will move out next month.
The other day I told them
I write poetry.

That is as intimate as men get.
We live across the hall.
We eat and watch together.
Someone dies.
We see we are alone.

THE CHILD

the child the child his sleeve was empty it
flapped obscenely as he ran—the child he ran
he ran right by

my car

my God

I thought that that child my God that poor child
God—my God—bless him.
and then
I saw
the bulge in his shirt where he had pulled his arm into
his sleeve—his empty sleeve
and—Oh My God—I sighed
and then
I was angry.
angry at the little bit of child—that boychild—that boy
who fooled me into feeling for him. who the hell
does he think he is, when the children without arms,
without legs—without lives—cannot hide themselves
and run around with empty sleeves, empty pants
empty beings—and then reappear whole?
My God, how can this be, this feeling?
blindly feeling my way through such darkness
so much darkness—feeling for this child that child
this boy—my girl—my God. who the hell
do You think You are to take my girl
and leave that wicked boy an arm to
grow back and all those other boys
and girls—oh You are God, that is Who and
it was not You who made the boy make me feel. it was not You
it was not You it was not You.

HOW DID YOU FEEL WHEN YOUR PRAYERS WERE NOT ANSWERED?

The nice lady in the grief group asked me.

To pray is to admit that there is someone
bigger than yourself
who listens.

To bargain is to believe
that there are values,
someone capable of making changes.

To argue and rage is to know
that what is right matters.

Lady, I cannot share your golden gates,
cloud palaces,
ever-afters.

I have only this:
I prayed, bargained,
and raged my best arguments
against the mistake that was made.

That is all I have.

THE ACCOUNTING

darkness	=	(light)			
(light)	=	void			
void	=	(everything)	=	nothing	
nothing	=	vacuum			
vacuum	+	anything	=	everything	
anything	+	(anything)	=	void	
	=	vacuum	=	(everything)	
words	=	power	>	void	
	>	darkness	>	Evil	.
power	>	(power)	=	nothing	
nothing	=	(God)			
(God)	=	Evil	=	void	
	=	(light)	=	darkness	

|||

Grief is born of love.

— Rabbi Jonathan Miller, *Travel Journal*

THE RABBI VISITS ASIA

1. Vietnam

Soldiers came to our village.
              You are Communists now.
Good, we said. *Now we will be safe.*
A week later my son stepped on a land mine.

The soldiers came back the next fall.
              You are the wrong kind of Communists.
              You must change.
Good, we said. *Being the other kind*
was not working very well.
A month later an old woman in our village starved.
My niece died for lack of medicine.

              The monks tell us it does not
              matter what we are.
              They say the same about our hunger.

The Americans came.
They brought food, medicine, tools.
              You are no longer Communists.
What are we? we asked.
              Free! They smiled.
We showed them the rice paddies,
the sky, the graves of our dead.
They did not understand.

2. Action

An owl took my cat.
              Now rats will eat our rice.
I found duck eggs this morning.
              They will make my daughters strong.

The stick that fell for me was death.
But when? I cannot be bothered.
I caught three fish today.

Tonight we will eat well.
We will apologize to the Duck, the Fish.
I will look for another cat tomorrow.

Let us put the children to bed
and walk beneath the stars
as the Owl thanks us for sharing this night.

3. Inaction

Every man has two hands
so he can hold and build.
Every man has two legs
so he will not fall to right or left.

Every man has two ears
so he can hear good when evil calls,
two eyes so he can see both sides.

Every man has two faces.
One looks out as he works,
builds destroys.
One looks in, the face
from which he cannot hide
the truth of himself.

At night when all outside things
appear the same,
he looks into himself
and asks his heart's forgiveness.

4. Lao Time

God made the world in seven days.
        He made man a maker.
                He made woman a maker.
        He did not tell them how many minutes
                were in an hour, how many hours in a day.

He may not have even made the minutes and hours
        until the eighth or ninth day,
                when He made cause and effect
        and set the world's engine
                to run though time on its own power.

I am more than a rabbi.
You are more than a mother.
        Our days on earth are measured in hours.
        Our lives are measured by more.
        They are what we make them.
        They are what we make.
        They make us what we are.

We are. We make.
In time, we will be more.

5. Shadow Puppets in Cambodia

There cannot be light without shadow.
We say the shadow is dark, the light good.
And yet sunlight causes cancer,
heat can kill. *What do we know?*

    Hitler killed half of our people.
    We will never recover our place in the world.
    Perhaps he will be proven successful.
    What do we know?

Joy is life.
Sadness is life.
We do not like sadness.
The alternative to sadness is not joy,
but death.

We *do not know* why this is so.
We only know how to make others happy
and safe in this world.
We learn to do this while we carry our sadness
and look for our joys.

6. Inaction in Action

For the sin we have sinned against You
by using violence to throw off oppression.
For the sin we have sinned against You
by appeasing oppressors.
For the sin we have sinned against You
by using evil means to achieve good ends.
For believing we can determine
which ends are good enough to warrant violence.

> The monks say nothing
> warrants such action.

> The rabbis say it is the action
> that matters most.

The Buddha taught
there is action
in inaction.

> Moses killed the overseer.

The Zen Masters say we cannot know
when we must act.

The sages say we may not find answers
but the questioning itself is sacred.

The Buddha taught
we must be mindful
of all things.

Heschel says our awareness
is one of God's greatest gifts.

For the sin of failing to be mindful and aware
of the suffering of the world
and the sin of thinking empathy is enough.
For the sin of lashing out in pain
and the sin of enduring in silence that which I can change.
For all these sins.
For all these sins.
For all these sins
I pray and I promise.

SHARE AND TELL

the child wants to be
        wants to be
                more than anything

so much
        that she plays
            at being

she will change
        what she wants to be
            tomorrow

a child
        by definition
            will never learn

young men
        want to be
            inside another

they are full of themselves
        wanting to empty
            wanting to consume

old men and animals
        just want to be
            and be left be

the lonely want to share
        without giving up
            what they have or might be

I want to be
        and to be more
            than anything

but not give up any
            thing I have
                    except this heaviness

that I would trade
            for a sunlight
                    we can share

even when we walk into darkness
            we would carry it
                    and it would carry us

HOPE IN DROWNING

For each of us a river,
        its flow the measure
                of our days.

kick
        drift
                scull

We swim
        or are swept.
                Which of these is love?

For each of us
        a river,

a seamless glissade
        of tears and sweat.

The arid
        plumbous body
                leaves no stain

even as
        we are surrendered
                to the sea,

where time ends
        and I would believe
                all waters meld.

KADDISH

You are gone and you are lost and I go on.
But I must know that even though I delay
I seek a way that you live on and we live on.
And together for all time we may be
joined hand to hand to share the dream that is life. *Amen.*

I may a ray of hope make from this: I found profound relief in prayer.
Your heart in mine and your soul in mine and your past life
and your love of life and your joy in life
and your old dreams and your new dreams say to me you live on
and I, too,
I live on in your love and you in my love
and in God's love and I know that love promises lives beyond life. *Amen.*

I pray that in His love and
my need to find God in this world
I find strength to believe. *Amen.*

> *Oh I pray for life in this world*
> *and for love in the world to come,*
> *that you and I may be together.* Amen.

THE RABBI VISITS INDIA

1. The Streets of India

The world is full of color.

      if there must be pain

The world is full of cymbals and bells.

      give it to me

The world is full of smells,
of feces and incense
of curry and sweat
of dust and diesel.

      if there must be pain give it to me

The world is full of people great and small,
begging and selling,
taking and giving.

All the garish splendor,
the cacophonies,
the joys, horrors, pain
and sorrow,
all the world sings Life! Life!

The children scream Life!
The cattle bellow Life!
The pus, the boils,
the begging and demanding,

the gods who listen and the gods who only smile.
And the gods, the gods
who exist only in the black hole
of world hopelessness

with arms
and heads
and fangs.

And Kali and Shiva
and the serpent and the mongoose

all scream Life! Life!

> *if there must be pain*

and there must,

> *let me take it*

that it be on my name,
my people, my place.

And by this let me live and feel and suffer and heal.
And by this let me know that I am alive
with the living others
for one more golden, fetid, beautiful day.

2. The Indians in India

Who's your people?

What is your place?

> In this crazy quilt of cerulean and crimson and saffron
> on these streets where the naked walk naked
> and palms are outstretched.

Who's your people?

What is your place?

Where is your home?

As you bump and amble
Brownian among the teeming brown people.

You scull through the river of men
to the temple to the horizon
and always, within yourself, Jew.

You are that you are.

Who by fire?

Who by rain?

Who by the swallowing beast of mankind?

Who's your people?

How shall I call you?

3. The Rabbi Visits the Taj Mahal

<u>*Taj*</u>

Her beauty rises to heaven, he writes,
unable to contain his admiration.
He sees life in sandstone and marble

beneath the glare of her dome.
Beggars and thieves
drag their souls through shadows
and feed and breathe
and will their hearts to piston out life.

A rabbi is trained to look to heaven
but to minister to the earth.

B'reshit

And God formed man...
vayitzer being misspelled: *vayyitzer.*
The *Zohar* says it is because we are of two natures.
Others say that we have one foot in heaven, one on earth.
Perhaps it is because man is a maker of things,
who must choose between ascendance
and the other alternatives.

Taj

What monument do we build to love?
Beyond spasm, dirt, feces,
dust, boils, hunger and need

      Oh I'm close I am so close!

the throb that is the miracle and the mundane
the beauty we hope but cannot name

      Oh please do not stop! Oh god ogodogod!

Dull flesh molded into, what?
The certainty of death and loss,
the reach beyond the albatross
of being and then abruptly, not.

What monument do we build
to a vacuum, to the children
we love into existence,
knowing they will slip from our fingers?

      Do not drop the baby,

that is all a father must do, that,
and pray that he is already dead
when she falls of her own weight.

The Akidah

No, it did not happen that way.
Sarah screamed and the slave woman
handed Abram the living miracle,
he of the smiling face,
unbelieving mother,
and bargained-for life.

And the child screamed
Life! Life! Life!

And Abram saw in its face eternity,
his life beyond time
all love all grief held
in the fragile grip of a tiny hand.

Bet Shekinah

None may speak the name of God
or bring him into flesh as a graven image.
What more is a word?
Or a building to house, what we cannot say?
All formed things fade and fall,
be they made of stone or breath.

I cannot write you back into this world
or curse myself beyond it.
I can only look up.

And pray, knowing it is not the words,
but need that tempers logic's harsh decree,
the hope I have to throw against
the fortress of logic.

That, and the sun and the sea,
the memory of your smile,
the sound of your sister's voice,
even the fact of this world and its end.
These things argue for us, my Darling.

Men reach to the root of pain
and find love.
We take solace in the world before us
as the works of our hands mimic
the promise that we are more
than the four corners of our bodies
and less than something more.

IV

Denied the beauty of life,
we find life in the beautiful.

— Barry Marks, *Journal from Andros Island Trip*

CERULEAN

Let me tell you about my day.

Three of us. The Old Man, his son, me.
The cab stuttered off from
Andros International Airport
(one runway, two hangars)
and immediately we see that he's driving
on the wrong side of the road.
Wrong as in British but also
because the car is American,
a Town Car
that craps out just before Fresh Creek.

We're here for the bones,
the ghost fish.
The Old Man demands it.
He can't say what he's thinking anymore
or he'd tell us that fishing for snapper or mahi
is like wasting it on the fluffer girl.

He used to talk like that.

> *Da bones, dey is da t'ing, Mon,*

he'd say,

> *They spook if you don't lay the fly*
> *just right then they hit the fly an' den*
> *run like a scalded dawg!*

He'd revert to just enough Atlanta
to remind you who he was.
Who he was.

> *Right. Left. They run crazy*
> *like bottle rockets. You remember*

that July 4th when I bent the fin
and got you to go out an' light it?

He'd turn to his son, laughing over
the treachery that was designed to teach
something about being a man.
Everything is about that between father and son
until the father fails
and it's exam time.

At least this got me
out of bed,
out of the house,
out of thinking of you suspended in the air.

•

This is what I know about Andros:
largest island in the Bahamas,
          once called *La Isla del Espirito Santo,*
sparsely populated,
great fishing.

Here, the sky is blue to match the water,
the water blue as the sky and both
blue as if we should live forever.
We dream we are swimming out
and then across the sky,
careful lest we fall out of bed,
straight through the ceiling.

•

But of course the Town Car dies
on the No Name Road and we wait
for the brother/cousin/friend
in the Malibu who inevitably shows up.

Why You Vex?

Asks the *Bahamian Times* column.

I vex because it's hot
and the driver is so cool.

No problem.
Steve, he comin'.

Dis car, Mahn. She go to da mainland,
to the States. And goodbye.
The Mennonites got her runnin'
but she done.
I come back wit' another.
I told my wife, Mon, this car—
she dead.

•

Frontotemporal Dementia—
Pick's Disease.
Very rare, especially in men.
Not thought to be contagious.
Strong genetic component.

If I could, I would ask the Old Man
if he feels trapped, locked inside
his bad luck, his four dozen words.
But how could he answer?
And where would that leave me?
I have had nothing to say for so long.

•

The guide almost smiles.
He of the
No, no, Mahn. Not so far back.

He of the

Give me d'pole. See?
One... TWO.
One... TWO.

And the fly obeys like it's his kid,

arcing balletic

backcast

and then the line

spools out,

gracefully drops,

so that the fly settles

like a fly

on the glassy surface.

See, Mahn?
One... TWO.
One... TWO.
Y'let the line load,
y'cannot force it.
One... TWO.
It loads and shoots.

Professor Lavendo, Ph.D. in bonefishing,
patiently hands the pole back
to the brain surgeon lawyer who's labored forty years
to be able to afford to fish with him.

It's all timing, Mahn.
            One...TWO.
            One...TWO.
            You see?
            You see d'fish dere?
            No, not dere, that jes' lemon shark.
            Dere. We wade out.
            C'mon.

            Cas' dere.
            Furtha.
            Nice.

            •

Supper at the Big House:
The Old Man, he's got maybe
fifty words. His favorite expressions
will be the last to go.
How much of him is trapped in there?
Don't know.
It's clear that he enjoys this:

            It's a beautiful day!

You want to go out after bonefish tomorrow or stay in? It may storm.

            Let's go up in 'ere an' get some.
            Some bones. Let's go.

Tomorrow.

            Tomorrow?
            I like it. I like that.

Good. Let's have dinner and we'll go out tomorrow after those bonies.

            Oh? We go up in 'ere and get some dinner?
            Up in 'ere?
            I like it.

Ya. The restaurant.
We can wash up first. Meet in an hour.

An hour? Up in 'ere?
Then some bones.

Tomorrow.

Bonefish tomorrow!
I like it.

It's clear that he enjoys this.
I can hear Lavendo's voice explain:

Y'don' have to say it, jes' feel it.
Don' t'ink about it, Mahn.
Feel it.

One... TWO.

It has nothing to do with words,
thought even.
The soul is an ear,
the heart is an eye.
What words truly
ever made men happy?

Bonefish tomorrow?
Tomorrow. I like that.
It's a beautiful day!

•

Where are we?
My buddy Doug used to tell of the ancient
Native American tribe that disappeared due to
a lack of a sense of direction.

The *Fahkawi.* As in
Where the *Fahkawi?*

We are here, in Andros.
On the corner of No Name Road
and Buccaneer Street. Or is it Third?
The signs are challenging, turned by wind,
errant drivers, kids bored with their permanent vacations.
Over there is the
First Church of God's Light Small Hope Bay
and beyond, *Z's One Stop,*
which is a mile past *Ma's Quickway*
and the unclaimed *Quick Stop,* just before
the improbably named *Ann's One Way.*
Cokes, bread, beer, bait.
What else could you need?
Maybe words for what is bugging you,
words you can put in a box
and toss overboard.
Davey Jones' Locker.

> *No Dav-ee Jones, Mahn.*
> *Lusca, him hit' de han's*
> *liv in de Blue Holes.*
> *Grab you, Mahn,*
> *down to de bottom.*
> *Hold you like a lova'*
> *den you drown*
> *an' de sea crob pick you clean.*

Maybe a legend, a funny name.
Maybe a new water pump
or a cousin with a Malibu.

•

The sky on day two is cloudy
but the water impossibly clear.
Hints that a front is coming:
wind and a touch of rain.

Lavendo has us in the lee
of an island. He explains
that the fishing will be good today,
awful tomorrow.

> *It's d'pressha.*
> *Not rain. Not light.*
> *When d'pressha drop,*
> *the fish go deep.*

Pressure drops…fish think they are too shallow,
too near the surface.
The surface, the edge of things
is where death lives.
Good for feeding but
sunlight
birds
sharks able to trap even the fastest
between their teeth and the not-water.
The strangeness of the not-water.

> *One…TWO.*

The sky is blue.

Or is it?
How blue? By what gauge?
Who is counting?
What words can describe all this?
What hymn can give comfort?
Where the *Fahkawi*, Dr. Heisenberg?

> *It's a beautiful day.*

What words?
The heart has no voice.
It cannot speak except through
the librarian upstairs.

And that bookish organ
wants to rename everything.

      Why are these islands and channels
      called the Jupiters?

              Because dey always have been, Mahn.

What do I know?
There is no perspective up close,
and myopia in the distance.
Lavendo says to cast
          furtha.
The book says 40 to 60 feet but
he can shoot the whole reel.
        How far is furtha?
I can't even cast 30 feet.

At home, most days it is so dark
I can't practice fly-casting in the park.
I read in bed with the light on,
curtains closed.
I keep the television on, always.
My mind wanders and, like a fish sensing danger,
snaps from images and memories,
runs deeper into darkness, then drifts,
drifts, nosing about the wreckage.

But on Andros, the sea is infused with light,
so clear I can see my toes as we wade.

        D'front is comin', Mahn.
        You can feel it in d'wind.

The air, humid, a few drops blown
from a distant cloud.

      Sky wet,
      sea bright.

Is heaven coming
to earth tonight?

•

Dey'll be bitin' now.
Feeding before d'go deep.
See? See dere?
Cas' now. No.
Furtha.
Nice.
Now, strip.
Strip d' line in.
Strip.
Yah, Mahn!

And everything stops, focuses.

The line sings through the reel.

Right he goes.

Left.

Out.

He comin' in! Reel now!
Yes, Mahn.
Now stop. Stop!
Let go.
Let 'im run.
He not ready t'come in.

Let go.
Focus, then let go.
Focus.

Now, he tired.
Good.

When you make him turn his head t'you
that mean he finish.

We will bring him close.
Lavendo reaches, holds.
I snap a picture and then
we release him quick,
before the sharks come.

The sharks.
Yellow shadows.
A glimpse of the silver body,
torpedo perfect.
Gasping.
Doomed.

Lavendo tosses him toward the mangrove
where just maybe he can make it in
before the sharks.

No.

A flurry in the water,
then peace.

    Sorry, Pal.

        Is d'smell.
        Even you wear gloves.
        He's tired and the sharks,
        they know man-smell.
        They can track 'im.

We wade back to the boat.
I eye a five-foot lemon, who seems
all too expectant and maybe too eager.

The front is coming in.
The edge of something.
Something is going to happen.

If the sky and sea are inverted,
maybe you are closer to me today.

•

Morphology of *bonefish:*

> Kingdom: *Animalia*
> Phylum: *Chordata*
> Class: *Actinopterygii*
> Order: *Albuliformes*
> Family: *Albulidae*
> Genus: *Albula*
> Species: *A. vulpes*

> > Actually, there are three bonefish species:

> > "The bonefish, also known as 'phantom' or 'gray ghost,'
> > is probably pound for pound the strongest and fastest moving
> > animal of any salt-water fish. Bonefishing is a deep-water
> > pursuit done in depths ranging from 18 to 88 feet
> > (5.5 to 27 m)."

> > Wrong.

> > But that is Wikipedia for you.

In Florida and the Bahamas,
bonefishing is strictly on the flats.
One to six feet, maybe.
They even *tail*, their tails out of the shallow water
as they nose the sand for crab and shrimp.

Morphology of *bonefish:*

rigid with bones for better swimming
inedible to white people
delicacy for sharks

> *You bake' em in foil*
> *and den pop 'em bones out.*
> *Dey good.*

Rigid for speed.
The human body, on the other hand
is flexible, contemplative
but only one organ
can make song, words, art,
can make itself known to the world.

And when it hardens,
the brain begins to die.
It can be surprisingly brittle,
like the back, which aches for rest
and the heart,
which has been known to shatter.

•

The seas are alive.
What fills the sky?

> *Aerial plankton.*

In the 20s, scientists believed that tiny bugs were blown
across the highways, a mile in the air in massive numbers.
"William Beebe, who pioneered deep-sea exploration…managed
to calculate that at least 186,000 insects had swept by him in
the first ninety minutes."
— Hugh Raffles, *Insectopedia*

Did Beebe later go looking for the same in his bathyscaphe?
A strata of blowing fishies in the sunless sea?
Insects and deep-sea monsters.
Poisonous spiders and jellyfish.

Tinier, deadlier.
Bacilli. Virus.

What is at the end of your line?
Care to dive in and find out?
Better to wade with the sharks, you know,
than to risk the bite of shadow.

What darkness waits above,
after the fall, tumbling amid screams
or a single major chord
into the ceiling?
Where did you go?
What whale, its maw stretched wide?
Will I find you there, like Pinocchio found Geppetto?
Monstro.
Remember, Sweetheart?
The image kept me up nights for years.
I never knew why.

•

It isn't fair.
Mute, stupid fish can fly, while I
am earthbound.
Like crabs and other bottom-feeders,
your father will only be borne aloft when
the sharks get me, or the invisible bugs.
Nothing is invisible,
only too small to see.

That is when we fly,
thrown to the sky by the current:
aerial plankton.
What rainbow promises
the naked sky will receive me?
Christians say their Jesus slept through
the storm he later quelled—I
am never so confident of sea or sky.

But fish mindlessly fly the liquid sky.
And Lavendo, Steve, Lux, Max'mus, Horace,
Z, Ma, Lucia, Janie: they get to fish
Conch Sound, Blanket Sound,
Stanyard Creek,
Small Hope,
up to the Jupiters
down to the Curly Cut Cays,
off Congo Town, the Bluff
Little Creek.
The bones get big
because they are loners.
In the north, off Lowe Sound,
they school in the Jupiter Cays.
Smaller, but the schools
are easier to track by sharks
and islanders. Their words are

One… TWO.

Their colors garish to speak
against the sea and sky.
And their hearts sing to themselves,
the music I can only guess.

Andros Island.
Rum and bonefish.
What is invisible
is too large to see.

Andros Island.
La Isla del Espirito Santo.
If so, the Holy Spirit works in strange ways.
The last thing on my mind
is the closest to my heart.

And closer for that.

AND RAINBOWS ARE REDUNDANT

the rain, the rain is falling from clouds that used to be invisible.
rain that used to be rain, then was lakes or rivers, puddles or gutter washes,
washing sewage and dirt down the drains past the dead things.
old things, plastic things, and rotted paper things are dead things, right? paper that
used to be trees but is still alive because
it is doing something—holding Moo Goo Gai Pan or groceries
or ink that holds thoughts,
and molecules are still molecules, perhaps other molecules
because matter and what matters can't die—
not like you.
you are dead, aren't you? isn't that what the doctor said?
what science says, as if you weren't matter.
but you were. you did—you do like the rain that makes my head wet,
and is the rain—the rain that is falling—
and then will be something else.
the rain that will also rise.

FINDING YOU
Lauren, 2010

…was sudden as a forest flower,
as the instant of waking,
as the moment a man first notices
      that the seasons have changed
      or that he is in love.

Finding you was finding myself.

When the light shines,
when the music stops,
when life is no longer
      a script written
      for another actor,
things become clear
and a father can learn.

Finding you was finding myself in you
and you in me
when I had given up looking
for either of us.

NOT THE NEWS

We're fine down here.
Your sister survived freshman year.
Your mother and John are still married.
I am no longer.
You already know all that.

I think of you every day.
Sometimes I do not cry.
But I suppose you know that, too.

Telling you this
is not reporting the news.
It has a lot in common
with prayer.

GRADUATION, MONTANA ACADEMY

Lost Prairie Road, Marion, MT

> *"And God divided the light from the darkness…*
> *And God made the firmament and divided the waters that were below*
> *the firmament from the waters that were above the firmament."*
> Genesis 1:3, 1:8

The road to Lost Prairie is white,
trees white, mountain, cloud, sky white,
tires and eyes slip in the sunlight white;
it is scary beautiful,
the way to Lost Prairie,
the way of the world.

White from white,
day from night.
Punch drunk from word drunk,
from just plain drunk.
The good sleep from the bad sleep,
the good death from the bad.

Step forward and ahead.
Separation is creation.
Separation is the way of the world.
And the world is told in twos.
And the world is white and dark and good.
And the world is white and dark and bad.

And the world is scary,
beautiful.

NOTES

Leah Ellen Marks was killed in an automobile accident five days after her seventeenth birthday, a passenger in a car driven by a young man impaired by drugs and alcohol. In a world of beautiful and talented children, she was gifted with undeniable beauty and talent. No poetry can do her justice.

Angels and Air is a reversal of Donne's *Air and Angels*, in which he extols the virtues of men's love as opposed to the less pure love of women.

The Rabbi Visits Asia and *The Rabbi Visits India* were inspired by the travel journals of Rabbi Jonathan Miller of Temple Emanuel, Birmingham, Alabama.

As to the Taj Mahal: Emperor Shah Jahan built the beautiful edifice in honor of his deceased wife, Mumatz Mahal.

B'reshit is the first word of the Torah ("In the beginning…"). It is true that the word for "made" is misspelled in the statement that God made man. Scholars have pondered this earliest typo for centuries.

The *Akidah* is the familiar and troubling tale of Abraham's instruction to sacrifice Isaac (whose name means "smiling face"). The miracle of Isaac's birth to the aged Sarah and Abraham was essential to God's promise that Abraham's descendants would be a great nation and owners of what is now Israel. Abraham's part of the bargain was to change his name from Abram, be circumcised, and obey God. As one who believes the Bible primarily allegorical, I offer this more realistic version of the story.

Bet Shekinah means "house of spirit." *Shekinah* is one of many words for the divine spirit, often used to connote God's female, mothering, or creative spirit. As is well known, only the High Priest knew the correct pronunciation of God's name and he only used it once a year during High Holy Day services. The greatest sin in Judaism, alongside murder, is idolatry.

Kaddish is an attempt to duplicate the rhythm and sound of the Jewish prayer recited by mourners and those expressing sympathy for them. It is not a translation of the actual prayer, which is in Aramaic rather than Hebrew. The prayer praises God and asks for peace; it never mentions death or the deceased, mourning or anything one would expect from a prayer recited by mourners. In fact, it is virtually identical to prayers recited at other times during services. Comfort for the mourners is to be found in recognition that death is the creation of a merciful God. No other promises are made.

Cerulean is based, with apologies to the other travelers, on an actual fishing trip. Andros Island is the largest and one of the least-inhabited islands in the Bahamas. It is an internationally recognized spot for bonefishing, one of the most challenging types of saltwater angling. Many of the locations named or described are actual spots on the island. The experience of bonefishing is captured as accurately as possible in the poem.

Frontotemporal Dementia, or Pick's Disease, is a debilitating, fatal illness in which portions of the brain cease to function, limiting the ability to use and later understand words in its earlier stages. My friend suffers from the disease.

For more information on Andros Island…go there.

Finding You and *Graduation*…—these poems were written to Lauren following Leah's death. Her struggle and triumph over many obstacles has resulted in a new and better life for her and her family.